The Hidden
TREASURE
That Lies In Plain Sight

*The Truth About The So Called Negroes
Of America and the 12 Tribes*

The Hidden
TREASURE
That Lies In Plain Sight

The Truth About The So Called Negroes
Of America and the 12 Tribes

Jeremy Shorter
www.jeremyshorter.net

AuthorHouse™ LLC
1663 Liberty Drive
Bloomington, IN 47403
www.authorhouse.com
Phone: 1-800-839-8640

© 2014 by Jeremy Shorter. All rights reserved.

No part of this book may be reproduced, stored in a retrieval system, or transmitted by any means without the written permission of the author.

Published by AuthorHouse   03/05/2014

ISBN: 978-1-4685-7430-2 (sc)
ISBN: 978-1-4685-7429-6 (hc)
ISBN: 978-1-4685-7428-9 (e)

Library of Congress Control Number: 2012905608

Any people depicted in stock imagery provided by Thinkstock are models, and such images are being used for illustrative purposes only.
Certain stock imagery © Thinkstock.

This book is printed on acid-free paper.

Because of the dynamic nature of the Internet, any web addresses or links contained in this book may have changed since publication and may no longer be valid. The views expressed in this work are solely those of the author and do not necessarily reflect the views of the publisher, and the publisher hereby disclaims any responsibility for them.

Contents

1   The Bible: A History Book of the So-Called Negros and the 12 Tribes..... 1
       Introduction.. 1

2   Who Are The Hebrew Israelites? 3
       The Covenant Between the Most High and Abraham 5
       Esau and Jacob 10
       12 Tribes 13
       The Color Of The Hebrew Israelites 15

3   The Curse 21
       Enslavement... 39
       A Remnant of Israel shall be saved... 42

4   Religion.. 45
       The Understanding Of John 3:16 57
       The Change Of The Sabbath 60

5   The Most High Chosen People 65
       Conclusion... 68

6	The Jewish People	69
	Conclusion	72
	The Star Of David Deception	73
7	Duty Of The Chosen People	77
	Conclusion	80

Preface

THIS BOOK GIVES biblical and historical information about the Biblical Hebrew Israelites (children of Israel/12 Tribes) and how the Most High made a covenant with them and they disobeyed him, thus causing the fall of them. I believe that the suffering and challenges that the so-called Negroes of America and the 12 Tribes did not happen accidentally. According to the Holy Bible it is all documented. Until the so called Negroes of America and the 12 Tribes around the world return to their true Nationality and acknowledge of the God of Israel, then can we become that mighty and powerful nation that we were in biblical times. I believe that this book will fill in the missing facts about the true identity and heritage of the so called Negroes of America and the 12 Tribes throughout the world. The real truth has been hidden, distorted and suppressed by the enemies of the Most High chosen people.

I have attempted to show and prove that the original people of the Bible were in fact a black people and the bible is their history book. My main reason for writing this book is to shed light upon this dark world filled with lies.

Moreover, I would like to express special thanks to the Most High, for feeding me wisdom, knowledge and understanding through his Son.

1

The Bible: A History Book of the So-Called Negros and the 12 Tribes

Introduction

THE BIBLE IS a history book of the original black Hebrew Israelites and the 12 Tribes who are the children of Israel. Throughout history they show the white European civilization as the first civilization. History has been handed down to the so called Negros (Hebrew Israelites) by false pictures of human history altered history and the cover up of the truth. One who is well learned in Ancient History will be able of see past the lies and see the truth to which Nationality of people the bible refers to.

The Bible gives reliable evidence of the History of the Black Hebrew Israelites and the 12 Tribes. The bible itself is a mystery book full of prophecies and future prophecies of the people mentioned in the book. Biblical history has shown that the children of Israel (Hebrew Israelites) are spread throughout the world. What we must understand is that the so called Negreos (Hebrew Israelites) people wrote the Bible and they wrote it showing their history culture, mission, and their connection with the Creator (The Most High). I must also point out that the Hebrew Israelites are the original Jews. The ancient Biblical definition of the word "Jew" is a member of the tribe of Judah name of Jacob's fourth son. World English Dictionary defines Jew as "a member of the Semitic people who claim descent from the ancient Hebrew who is referred to as "Jews" one must engage in an in depth study of the Bible and research history.

Because of their disobedient to not keeping the laws and statutes of the Most High they fell as a nation and were dispersed throughout the four corners of the world. This ultimately caused them to forget their heritage as a Great people. Later on in the book I will discuss the color of the Hebrew Israelites and their duty as the Most High chosen people.

2

Who Are The Hebrew Israelites?

THE BIBLE GIVES us reliable evidence of the ancestry of the ancient Hebrew Israelites. The history of the Hebrew Israelites begins in Genesis 11:10 where the genealogy of Shem is recorded. The ancestry of the Hebrew Israelites stems from Abraham, who was a Hebrew Israelites, and black (Genesis 14:13). Although the Egyptians were a Black race, we must understand that they are from the descendants of Ham. In the tenth chapter of Genesis this can be proven. The Hebrew Israelites are a Holy nation and above all the other nation on the face of the earth. This is recorded in Deuteronomy chapter seven.

> *Deuteronomy 7:6-8 For thou art an holy people unto the Lord thy God: the Lord thy God hath chosen thee to be a special people unto himself, above all people that are upon the face of the earth.*

7 The Lord did not set his love upon you, nor choose you, because ye were more in number than any people; for ye were the fewest of all people:

8 But because the Lord loved you, and because he would keep the oath which he had sworn unto your fathers, hath the Lord brought you out with a mighty hand, and redeemed you out of the house of bondmen, from the hand of Pharaoh king of Egypt.

The children of Israel are The Most High's chosen people. They hold the keys to salvation to those Gentiles who accept the truth about the God of Israel and his chosen people. During the time while the black Israelites were in Egypt, the black Egyptians enslaved them. I will talk more about this later on in the book. Jesus (Yashaya) was also a black man, although the white religious institution portrays him as white. The messiah was also a Jew from the tribe of Judah. This can be pointed out in this following scripture:

John 4:9-10 then saith the woman of Samaria unto him, How is it that thou, being a Jew, askest drink of me, which am a woman of Samaria? for the Jews have no dealings with the Samaritans.

10 Jesus answered and said unto her, If thou knewest the gift of God, and who it is that saith to thee, Give me to drink; thou wouldest have asked of him, and he would have given thee living water.

The women of Samaria said unto the Messiah, "How is it that thou, being a Jew, askest drink of me, which am a woman of Samaria? For the Jews have no dealings with the Samaritans". This shows us that the Messiah was a Jew, because the women said "How is it that thou, being a Jew," She clearly knew that the Messiah was a Jew. Also the word Jew comes from the tribe of Judah as I stated earlier in this chapter. By us identifying what Nationality the Messiah was we can now identify his color. According to the 12 tribes the tribe of Judah is the so called Negroes of America who are Black and from the seed of Abraham.

As I pointed out that the messiah was from the tribe of Judah and this can be shown in this scripture:

> **Hebrews 7:14 For it is evident that our Lord sprang out of juda: of which tribe Moses spake nothing concerning priesthood.**

The foregoing information substantiates that the Hebrew Israelites and the prophets of the Bible were all black. Also we must understand that the so called Negros of America isn't African-Americans, but decedents of the Ancient Hebrew Israelites. Also to point out that the Africans enslaved the Hebrew Israelites, I will show this later on in the book.

The Covenant Between the Most High and Abraham

The Most High makes a covenant with Abraham and his seed. This covenant is very important when you read about Esau and Jacob and how religious institution make Jacob look like the bad guy and make him look like he stole Esau birthright. It's very important to understand the covenant that the Most High God made with Abraham. Shem is the genealogy of the children of Israel as stated in (Genesis 10:11) where the genealogy of Shem is recorded. Abraham was a Hebrew Israelites and came from the genealogy of Shem, and this is pointed out in this scripture:

> **Genesis 14:13 And there came one that had escaped, and told Abram the Hebrew; for he dwelt in the plain of Mamre the Amorite, brother of Eshcol, and brother of Aner: and these were confederate with Abram.**

In Chapter 15 the Most High God makes a covenant with Abraham. In Genesis 15:13 this is proof that the children of Israel (12 Tribes) are the Most High chosen people, and this also lets us know that Jacob had the promises already before Esau. Jacob comes from the seed of Abraham and Jacob is the father of the 12 Tribes which make up the children of Israel. The Most High said *"Know of a surety that thy seed shall be a stranger in a land that is not theirs, and shall serve them; and they shall afflict them four hundred years"*. This is pointed out in the following scriptures, read the precepts for understanding:

> **Genesis 15:12-13 And when the sun was going down, a deep sleep fell upon Abram; and, lo, an horror of great darkness fell upon him.**
>
> **13 And he said unto Abram, Know of a surety that thy seed shall be a stranger in a land that is not theirs, and shall serve them; and they shall afflict them four hundred years;**

Precept to Genesis 15:13:

> *Exodus 1:1 Now these are the names of the children of Israel, which came into Egypt; every man and his household came with Jacob.*

> *Exodus 1:11 Therefore they did set over them taskmasters to afflict them with their burdens. And they built for Pharaoh treasure cities, Pithom and Raamses.*

> *Exodus 12:40 Now the sojourning of the children of Israel, who dwelt in Egypt, was four hundred and thirty years.*

In that same day the Most High made a covenant with Abraham to give his seed a land, this is shown in the following scriptures:

> *Genesis 15:18-21 In the same day the LORD made a covenant with Abram, saying, Unto thy seed have I given this land, from the river of Egypt unto the great river, the river Euphrates:*

> *19 The Kenites, and the Kenizzites, and the Kadmonites,*

> *20 And the Hittites, and the Perizzites, and the Rephaims,*

21 And the Amorites, and the Canaanites, and the Girgashites, and the Jebusites.

In Genesis 17 the Most High makes another covenant with him and tells him *"he will multiply thee exceedingly and he shall be a father of many nations (12 Tribes) and he also tells him that Kings shall come out of thee"*. The Most High promise Abraham that he would be the father of many nations, this will be done through the seed of Abraham, Isaac, and Jacob who is the father of the 12 Tribes. This can be shown in the following scriptures:

> **Genesis 17:1-9 And when Abram was ninety years old and nine, the LORD appeared to Abram, and said unto him, I am the Almighty God; walk before me, and be thou perfect.**
>
> **2 And I will make my covenant between me and thee, and will multiply thee exceedingly.**
>
> **3 And Abram fell on his face: and God talked with him, saying,**
>
> **4 As for me, behold, my covenant is with thee, and thou shalt be a father of many nations.**
>
> **5 Neither shall thy name any more be called Abram, but thy name shall be Abraham; for a father of many nations have I made thee.**

6 And I will make thee exceeding fruitful, and I will make nations of thee, and kings shall come out of thee.

7 And I will establish my covenant between me and thee and thy seed after thee in their generations for an everlasting covenant, to be a God unto thee, and to thy seed after thee.

8 And I will give unto thee, and to thy seed after thee, the land wherein thou art a stranger, all the land of Canaan, for an everlasting possession; and I will be their God.

9 And God said unto Abraham, Thou shalt keep my covenant therefore, thou, and thy seed after thee in their generations.

In Genesis chapter 17 the Most High makes an everlasting covenant with Abraham son who is Isaac and with his seed after him. This is shown in these scriptures:

Genesis 17:19-20 And God said, Sarah thy wife shall bear thee a son indeed; and thou shalt call his name Isaac: and I will establish my covenant with him for an everlasting covenant and with his seed after him.

20 And as for Ishmael, I have heard thee: Behold, I have blessed him, and will make him fruitful, and will multiply him exceedingly; twelve princes shall he beget, and I will make him a great nation.

In Genesis chapter 21 Sarah conceived and had Isaac, this pointed out in these scriptures:

> **Genesis 21:2-3 For Sarah conceived, and bare Abraham a son in his old age, at the set time of which God had spoken to him.**
>
> **3 And Abraham called the name of his son that was born unto him, whom Sarah bare to him, Isaac.**

This covenant that the father made with Abraham is very important when understanding Esau and Jacob fight over the birthright in the womb, and understanding how Jacob already had the promises.

Esau and Jacob

Isaac wife Rebekah conceives and has Esau and Jacob. According to the Bible you are what your father is (Ezra 2:59.) The Most High said *"Two nations are in thy womb, and two manner of people shall be separated from thy bowels"*. Nation is short for Nationality. They weren't identical twins. The Most high speaks to Rebekah in this manner:

> **Genesis 25:21-34 And Isaac intreated the LORD for his wife, because she was barren: and the LORD was intreated of him, and Rebekah his wife conceived.**

22 And the children struggled together within her; and she said, If it be so, why am I thus? And she went to enquire of the LORD.

23 And the LORD said unto her, Two nations are in thy womb, and two manner of people shall be separated from thy bowels; and the one people shall be stronger than the other people; and the elder shall serve the younger.

24 And when her days to be delivered were fulfilled, behold, there were twins in her womb.

25 And the first came out red, all over like an hairy garment; and they called his name Esau.

26 And after that came his brother out, and his hand took hold on Esau's heel; and his name was called Jacob: and Isaac was threescore years old when she bare them.

27 And the boys grew: and Esau was a cunning hunter, a man of the field; and Jacob was a plain man, dwelling in tents.

28 And Isaac loved Esau, because he did eat of his venison: but Rebekah loved Jacob.

29 And Jacob sod pottage: and Esau came from the field, and he was faint:

30 And Esau said to Jacob, Feed me, I pray thee, with that same red pottage; for I am faint: therefore was his name called Edom.

31 And Jacob said, Sell me this day thy birthright.

32 And Esau said, Behold, I am at the point to die: and what profit shall this birthright do to me?

33 And Jacob said, Swear to me this day; and he sware unto him: and he sold his birthright unto Jacob.

34 Then Jacob gave Esau bread and pottage of lentiles; and he did eat and drink, and rose up, and went his way: thus Esau despised his birthright.

In Verse 23 it says one "*one people shall be stronger than the other people*"**,** meaning you would have one people more physical strong and spiritual strong. According to Genesis 15:13 this lets us know that the promise was already given to Jacob because Jacob is from Shem and Jacob is the Father of the 12 Tribes who will sojourn in that strange land, which is Egypt. Esau is the father of the Edomites you can read this in Genesis 36:1-43. That's why in Genesis 25:23 it said "*Two nations are in thy womb, and two manner of people shall be separated from thy bowels*". Then it goes on to say in verse 25 "*And the first came out red, all over like an hairy garment; and they called his name Esau.*" It says red because the blood show forth through the skin and in today's society that would be the Europeans or what we call the White Caucasian. There is no such thing as Black people, Black is a color, but there is such a thing as Brown people like unto the color of the ground.

And there is no such thing as white people; White is a color like the color of white printing paper. Esau was one of the sons of Isaac and the first born, meaning the first one that came out. In Genesis 25:23 it said that the elder would serve the younger brother, this lets us know that the promise was already given to Jacob before he was born. Jacob is the son of the promise and he is the one that the Most High promised that Esau would serve, that's why they were fighting in the womb. In 2 Esdras chapter six it tells us that Esau is the end of the world and Jacob is the beginning of the one that follows it. At the end of the world, meaning the end times which we are in. Esau is the end of the world. Meaning we will rule forever. You must ask yourself this, who is over the world today, what Nationality or group of people? It's the White Caucasian. Here are the scripture to prove this:

> **2 Esdras 6:8-9 And he said unto me, From Abraham unto Isaac, when Jacob and Esau were born of him, Jacob's hand held first the heel of Esau.**
>
> **9 For Esau is the end of the world, and Jacob is the beginning of it that followeth.**—*1611 KJV Bible (Apocrypha)*

12 Tribes

Jacob fathered 12 sons (Genesis 49:1-28). They are the ancestors of the tribes of Israel, and the ones for whom the tribes are named. The sons of Joseph, Ephraim and Manasseth, were given the status of independent tribes. Each occupied a separate territory (Numbers 34:1-29), except the tribe of Levi, which was set apart to serve in the Holy Temple (Numbers 18:24). These are the 12 Tribes of Israel: Reuben, Simeon, Levi, Judah, Zebulon, Issachar, Gad, Asher, Napthali,

Ephraim, Manasseth, Benjamin. At this point, I would like to explain to the readers that Jerusalem was the birthplace of us all (Galatians 4:26). The 12 Tribes of Israel today can be identified as the following:

Reuben—So called Seminole Indians/Aboriginal Australians

Simeon—So called Dominicans

Levi—So called Haitians

Judah—So called African Americans/Negroes

Zebulon—Guatemalans/Panamanians

Issachar—So called Mexicans

Gad—So called North American Indians

Asher—Columbians/Brazilians/Argentines/Venezuelans

Napthali—Hawaiians/Samoans/Tongans/Fijians

Ephraim—So called Puerto Ricans

Manasseth—So called Cubans

Benjamin—So called Jamaicans/Trinidadians/Guyanese

The 12 Tribes of Israel are the Most High people forever. This is shown in these scriptures:

> *I Chronicles 17:21-22 And what one nation in the earth is like thy people Israel, whom God went to redeem to be his own people, to make thee a name of greatness and terribleness, by driving out nations from before thy people, whom thou hast redeemed out of Egypt.*
>
> *22 For thy people Israel didst thou make thine own people for ever; and thou, LORD, becamest their God.*

The Color Of The Hebrew Israelites

For years, scholars, theologians and archaeologist have debated the answer to the question, "How did the ancient Hebrew Israelites people look physically? My research has leaded me to confirm that although the scriptures and other historical documents have left a lot of evidence that confirms the physical appearance of the Hebrew Israelites people. Most religious institution teach that the people in Israel today known as "Ashkenazi Jews or Jewish People" are the direct descendants of the ancient Israelites, because they proclaim themselves to be the real Jews. The people today over in Israel are not the real Jews neither do they look like the Hebrew Israelites (children of Israel), they are white Europeans. The Europeans had a reason to lie and to cover up the truth to develop a white supremacy. They lied about the truth about how the Hebrew Israelites looked like, when they made it illegal for a black man and women to learn how to read during slavery times. They knew how holy the children of Israel were. I will talk more about the Jewish people and who they are further in the book.

The Bible tells us and shows us the color of the Hebrew Israelites. Many will argue up and down or say that color doesn't matter when it really does. We didn't make it a color issue the white Europeans made it one when they started to paint all the images white during the renaissance period. The Bible is a history book of the children of Israel. Throughout scripture Israel is described as physically looking like the sons of Ham in appearance. Ham was one of Noah's three sons, Shem and Japheth were the other two (Genesis 9:18). Noah's descendants repopulated the earth after the Great Flood. Ham's descendants are traced to the families of Africa. Ham in Hebrew means Black, hot and burnt. Egypt was traditionally called "the Land of Ham," and Ham was considered to be the ancestor of the Egyptians and of all African peoples south of Egypt. The Hebrew Israelites are descendants of Noah son Shem, through Abraham; he is the father of the Hebrew Israelite Nation. Abraham is the father of Isaac, Isaac is the father of Jacob, Jacob had twelve sons and these sons are the progenitors of the Israelite nation.

Joseph was one of the twelve sons of Jacob. Jacob sired Joseph in his old age, and he was clearly his favorite son. This caused Joseph's brothers to become jealous of him. Their jealousy resulted in Joseph being sold by Arab merchants as a slave to Egyptians (Genesis 37:3-36). Joseph became governor of Egypt and was second in command to Pharaoh in authority (Genesis 41:40-41 and Genesis 42:6). There was a famine in Canaan, where Jacob and his sons lived. Pharaoh had a dream which Joseph interpreted. His dream told of the forthcoming famine and gave Egypt an opportunity to prepare by storing food.) So, Jacob sent his ten sons to Egypt to buy bread. When Joseph's ten brothers came into Egypt they were brought before him. Joseph recognized his brothers, but they didn't recognize him, this is can be pointed out in the following scriptures:

> *Genesis 42:1-8 now when Jacob saw that there was corn in Egypt, Jacob said unto his sons, Why do ye look one upon another?*
>
> *2 And he said, Behold, I have heard that there is corn in Egypt: get you down thither, and buy for us from thence; that we may live, and not die.*
>
> *3 And Joseph's ten brethren went down to buy corn in Egypt.*
>
> *4 But Benjamin, Joseph's brother, Jacob sent not with his brethren; for he said, Lest peradventure mischief befall him.*
>
> *5 And the sons of Israel came to buy corn among those that came: for the famine was in the land of Canaan.*
>
> *6 And Josep0h was the governor over the land, and he it was that sold to all the people of the land: and Joseph's brethren came, and bowed down themselves before him with their faces to the earth.*
>
> *7 And Joseph saw his brethren, and he knew them, but made himself strange unto them, and spake roughly*

unto them; and he said unto them, Whence come ye? And they said, From the land of Canaan to buy food.

8 And Joseph knew his brethren, but they knew not him.

Since the ancient Egyptians were a black people, Joseph had to be black also. Joseph brothers would have recognized him easily among the "black" Egyptians. But Joseph's own flesh and blood brothers thought he was an Egyptian. Scripture tells us that Moses killed an Egyptian, after he saw him mistreating a Hebrew Israelite. So Moses had to flee from the land of Egypt for his life, because Pharaoh found out and sought to kill him. Pharaoh was trying to kill Moses because he found out Moses was a Hebrew and not his flesh and blood grandson (Exodus 2:12-15). Moses fled to the land of Midian (located in Saudi Arabia) where he helped seven daughters of the priest of Midian water their flock, after chasing away some bully shepherds. The girls went home to their father, Reuel and told him what happened:

Exodus 2:16-19 Now the priest of Midian had seven daughters: and they came and drew water, and filled the troughs to water their father's flock.

17 And the shepherds came and drove them away: but Moses stood up and helped them, and watered their flock.

18 And when they came to Reuel their father, he said, How is it that ye are come so soon to day?

19 And they said, An Egyptian delivered us out of the hand of the shepherds, and also drew water enough for us, and watered the flock.

Notice they didn't say a Hebrew in Egyptian clothing saved us; they described Moses as a black-skinned descendant of Ham (Egyptian). Further proof that Moses was "black" can be found in Exodus 4:6-7, in this passage, AHAYAH, (The Creator's name in Hebrew) is showing Moses a miracle so that he can prove to the children of Israel who sent him. This can be shown in these scriptures:

Exodus 4:6 And the LORD said furthermore unto him, Put now thine hand into thy bosom. And he put his hand into his bosom: and when he took it out, behold, his hand was leprous as snow.

7 And he said, Put thine hand into thy bosom again. And he put his hand into his bosom again; and plucked it out of his bosom, and, behold, it was turned again as his other flesh.

In verse 7 it says, The Lord told Moses to put his hand back into his bosom, and it turned as his other flesh. Meaning that the rest of his body (skin) was other than white or the opposite of white, which is black. Also notice in verse 6 when the Most High turned Moses hand to leprous as snow, and we all know that the color of snow is white. Then he turns his skin back again to his other (own) flesh which was black. Moses was a Hebrew Israelites from the tribe of Lev. This also shows us that Paul was mistaken for an Egyptian, although they were Black, they weren't from Shem as the Israelites were.)

3

The Curse

THE SO CALLED Black people of America are the true descendants of the Ancient Hebrew Israelites mentioned in the Bible. I also find that the curses mentioned in the Bible refer directly to the Blacks in America today and the 12 Tribes of Israel. Although the children of Israel were the chosen people of the Most High and were chosen to be a light to the Gentiles, but they were a rebellious nation. The scripture tells us to show his people (children of Israel) their transgression and the house of Jacob their sins. Here are some scripture that depicts the behavior of the children of Israel:

> **Hosea 4:6 My people are destroyed for lack of knowledge: because thou hast rejected knowledge, I will also reject thee, that thou shalt be no priest to me: seeing thou hast forgotten the law of thy God, I will also forget thy children.**

It's said "My people are destroyed for lack of knowledge. Notice it says my people, that people or nation is the 12 Tribes or the children of Israel. This can be proven in *Exodus 3:10*. They have been cut off by the Most High because we lack knowledge. They lack knowledge of the God of Israel who saved their forefather from the Egyptians. That's why in today's society their children are lost majority of their young teenagers are in jail and that's because the Most High has forgotten their children. The children of Israel have forgotten the law of the Most High that he gave unto their forefathers. Today in these so called Churches they preach we don't have to keep the law and that it's done away with, that's a lie, and we are to keep the laws of the Most High forever.

> **Zechariah 7:11-12 But they refused to hearken, and pulled away the shoulder, and stopped their ears, that they should not hear.**
>
> **12 Yea, they made their hearts as an adamant stone, lest they should hear the law, and the words which the Lord of hosts hath sent in his spirit by the former prophets: therefore came a great wrath from the Lord of hosts.**

Notice it said they. In today's society getting the children of Israel to understand who they are and their true Nationality is nearly impossible. When someone tries to present this truth to the 12 tribes by telling them who they are and that cargo slaves ships are mentioned in the bible they will immediately cut you off and turn away their shoulder, stop their ears, and keeping on walking. That's why it goes on to say "they made their hearts as an adamant stone" meaning they have harden their hearts. They refuse to hear his laws and the Most High words which he sent by his spirit by the former prophets, and that's why it goes on to say "therefore came a great wrath from the Most High of hosts". This is why you see the children of Israel at the bottom. Majority of them are in jail, and many of them have diseases like high blood pressure, and many more. Continue to read Zechariah 7:13-14.

> **Ezekiel 2:3-5 And he said unto me, Son of man, I send thee to the children of Israel, to a rebellious nation that hath rebelled against me: they and their fathers have transgressed against me, even unto this very day.**
>
> **4 For they are impudent children and stiffhearted. I do send thee unto them; and thou shalt say unto them, Thus saith the Lord GOD.**
>
> **5 And they, whether they will hear, or whether they will forbear, (for they are a rebellious house,) yet shall know that there hath been a prophet among them.**

The Hebrew Israelites are a rebellious people. Just look at the so called Blacks and the other 12 tribes today. You have children cursing out their parents; the children are over their parents it's just all out of order. The children of Israel have rebelled against the Father and have violated his laws until this very day. So why in these so called churches they teach that the Most High people don't have to keep the law? That is a lie; they are to keep the law as I already mentioned. They are disrespectful children as a nation.

Because of their disobedience, the Most High scattered the children of Israel throughout the different parts of the world and brought evil against them, this is foretold in the prophecies of the Holy Scripture. All the curses are to fit the Jews who are the so called Negros or what society calls the African-American and the 12 Tribes. I will explain the curse that fell upon the children of Israel mentioned in Deuteronomy chapter 28 below:

> **Deuteronomy 28:15 But it shall come to pass, if thou wilt not hearken unto the voice of the LORD thy God, to observe to do all his commandments and his statutes which I command thee this day; that all these curses shall come upon thee, and overtake thee:**

> **Deuteronomy 28:16 Cursed shalt thou be in the city, and cursed shalt thou be in the field.**

If you look at any "inner city" in the United States, you will find death and destruction like nowhere else. Many of these cities look like they belong in any war-torn country, they're devastated. These cities are largely populated by "African Americans", as this is where the majority of "blacks" in the United States live. Wherever you find a large population of "Blacks" living in rural/country areas, you will find the same death and destruction like you find in the urban city areas.

> **Deuteronomy 28:17 Cursed shall be thy basket and thy store.**

> **Deuteronomy 28:18 Cursed shall be the fruit of thy body, and the fruit of thy land, the increase of thy kine, and the flocks of thy sheep.**

These curses are going to follow the so-called "Blacks", for as long as they continue to sin against the Most High.

> ***Deuteronomy 28:20 The LORD shall send upon thee cursing, vexation, and rebuke, in all that thou settest thine hand unto for to do, until thou be destroyed, and until thou perish quickly; because of the wickedness of thy doings, whereby thou hast forsaken me.***

Just about everything "African Americans" have tried to do to improve their living conditions as a people, has failed. They have tried the political system (voting), the educational system (attaining college degrees), and economics (capitalism). But all these genres have been useless to them.

> ***Deuteronomy 28:21 The LORD shall make the pestilence cleave unto thee, until he have consumed thee from off the land, whither thou goest to possess it.***

> ***Deuteronomy 28:22 The LORD shall smite thee with a consumption, and with a fever, and with an inflammation, and with an extreme burning, and with the sword, and with blasting, and with mildew; and they shall pursue thee until thou perish.***

Verse 22 is referring to diseases and Lynching (killings). One of the worst episodes, of the life of a slave was the middle passage, the voyage from West Africa to the Americas. The conditions on the slave ships were unbearable; two to four hundred captives were packed like sardines in the bottom of the ships.

> *Deuteronomy 28:23 And thy heaven that is over thy head shall be brass, and the earth that is under thee shall be iron*
>
> *Deuteronomy 28:24 The LORD shall make the rain of thy land powder and dust: from heaven shall it come down upon thee, until thou be destroyed.*
>
> *Deuteronomy 28:25 The LORD shall cause thee to be smitten before thine enemies: thou shalt go out one way against them, and flee seven ways before them: and shalt be removed into all the kingdoms of the earth*

In verse 25 it *clearly* tells us that Israel (12 Tribes) is to be smitten/defeated by their enemies. Also In verse 25 it clearly tell us that Israel will be removed into all the kingdoms of the earth, meaning they are to be spread throughout the 4 corners of the world. The word Smitten means grievously or disastrously stricken or afflicted.

> *Deuteronomy 28:26 And thy carcase shall be meat unto all fowls of the air, and unto the beasts of the earth, and no man shall fray them away.*
>
> *Deuteronomy 28:27 The LORD will smite thee with the botch of Egypt, and with the emerods, and with the scab, and with the itch, whereof thou canst not be healed.*

Deuteronomy 28:28 The LORD shall smite thee with madness, and blindness, and astonishment of heart:

The so called African Americans (Hebrew Israelites/Jews) are in a deep, deep spiritual darkness, they have become ignorant and unaware of the truth about their heritage and their Creator, who is the God of Israel, AHAYAH ASHAR AHAYAH in Hebrew and in English I AM THAT I AM (Exodus 3:14). Instead, they have embraced the slave master's religion, doctrines and culture, not realizing that it was under the auspices of his religion that they were enslaved. The so called Negreos state of madness and blindness has caused them to be astonished at our own condition. They are perplexed as to why they seem to be the most hated of all races of men on the face of the earth. They are always the target of discrimination, racism or police brutality. Rodney King, Emit Till, James Byrd Jr. and Ricky Byrdsong, only represent a few of the thousands of victims who have been raped, lynched, beaten, shot and murdered for no apparent reason other than their "racial" identity

Deuteronomy 28:29 And thou shalt grope at noonday, as the blind gropeth in darkness, and thou shalt not prosper in thy ways: and thou shalt be only oppressed and spoiled evermore, and no man shall save thee.

The above scripture is saying that Israel is going to grope, which means to search around with uncertainty or blindly search. A blind man lives in a world of darkness, and he is forced to grope in order to navigate his surroundings. The scripture also says that no man shall save the children of Israel. The so called Negros has in their history countless men and women who have tried to save this people. Men such as: Frederick Douglass, Nat Turner, Marcus Garvey, Malcolm X, Elijah Muhammad, and a host of others. Freedom will only come through a "spiritual" awakening and healing of the problem that causes our captivity and prolongs our continued oppression. They must come back to the Most High, the God of Israel, and the Creator.

> **Deuteronomy 28:30 Thou shalt betroth a wife, and another man shall lie with her: thou shalt build an house, and thou shalt not dwell therein: thou shalt plant a vineyard, and shalt not gather the grapes thereof.**

Everything Israel has is going to be taken or belong to someone else. Once again scripture is describing their situation in the West. During slavery, slave owners often took the wives of "Black" (Hebrew Israelites/Jews) slaves and slept with them. This happened during the middle passage, and after the slaves arrived on land.

> **Deuteronomy 28:31 Thine ox shall be slain before thine eyes, and thou shalt not eat thereof: thine ass shall be violently taken away from before thy face, and shall not be restored to thee: thy sheep shall be given unto thine enemies, and thou shalt have none to rescue them.**

> **Deuteronomy 28:32 Thy sons and thy daughters shall be given unto another people, and thine eyes shall look, and fail with longing for them all the day long: and there shall be no might in thine hand**

Black families were ripped apart during the long harsh period of the Atlantic slave trade. In some instances, the sons and daughters of "blacks" were captured while away from their parents, never to see them again. In other cases, entire families were taken into captivity, where parents often watched their children sold to different slave masters and different plantations. In the year 2002 on the local news in Chicago (fox news), they presented a special report called *'The Forgotten Children'*. In this special they were showing how Northern Europeans and some Canadians are adopting black children in Mass. These children were removed from their black parents and given to these other people overseas. The report was shocking, but very informative.

> ***Deuteronomy 28:33 The fruit of thy land, and all thy labors, shall a nation which thou knowest not eat up; and thou shalt be only oppressed and crushed always:***

Because "African Americans" have seen so much discrimination, racism, hatred and death directed toward them, that is has literally driven many of us crazy, to the point that we are filling up the mental institutions in this country. They are also being diagnosed younger, and more often with mental illness than any other racial group in the United States.

> ***Deuteronomy 28:35 The LORD shall smite thee in the knees, and in the legs, with a sore botch that cannot be healed, from the sole of thy foot unto the top of thy head.***

> ***Deuteronomy 28:36 The LORD shall bring thee, and thy king which thou shalt set over thee, unto a nation***

> ***which neither thou nor thy fathers have known; and there shalt thou serve other gods, wood and stone.***

It's not a coincidence that this part of the world was known as the 'NEW WORLD' and this is the land that the Hebrew Israelites ("So called Negros") was brought into as captives, along with their self-appointed kings. They were brought, to a nation neither them nor their fathers knew about. A nation that was not known to the entire world until thousands of years after this prophecy was written. In verse 36 it also says that they are going to worship gods (other religions) of wood and stone. Every religion has a god or gods, so in this verse "gods" also means the various religions. Christianity has Wood Cross and Muslim the Kaaba/Black Stone.

> ***Deuteronomy 28:37 And thou shalt become an astonishment, a proverb, and a byword, among all nations whither the LORD shall lead thee.***

The general attitudes of some "black" people are so disgraceful that it motivates other races to observe them with astonishment. This is the reason many people are always asking the question "why are blacks behind"? "They should be ahead of other groups since they have been here for over 400 years". Proverbs and bywords are nicknames that are used in a scornful manner in substitution for our true nationality. Since the time that the so called Negros have gotten off the slave ships and was brought to America they have been called all types of proverb and bywords. Excuse the language, but here are some bywords: Nigger, Nigga, Monkey, Coon, Porch Money, Gorilla Face, and Dirty.

Deuteronomy 28:38 Thou shalt carry much seed out into the field, and shalt gather but little in; for the locust shall consume it.

Deuteronomy 28:39 Thou shalt plant vineyards, and dress them, but shalt neither drink of the wine, nor gather the grapes; for the worms shall eat them.

Deuteronomy 28:40 Thou shalt have olive trees throughout all thy coasts, but thou shalt not anoint thyself with the oil; for thine olive shall cast his fruit.

Deuteronomy 28:41 Thou shalt beget sons and daughters, but thou shalt not enjoy them; for they shall go into captivity.

The bible tells us that ancient Israel went into much captivity (Egypt, Assyria, Babylon etc.). But this is exactly how they Hebrew Israelites got here; our fore parents were brought to this part of the world as captive slaves. Who were captured on the west coast of Africa? This isn't how the Jews (the so called Negreos) or any other ethnic group got here. All other groups came here on their own free will.

Deuteronomy 28:43 The stranger that is within thee shall get up above thee very high; and thou shalt come down very low.

In this verse 43, stranger refers to other ethnic / racial groups other than the children of Israel. This means that other racial / ethnic groups that live in the same country or city as the Hebrews Israelites will rise up the social / economic ladder higher than the children of Israel, as a collective people.

> **Deuteronomy 28:44 He shall lend to thee, and thou shalt not lend to him: he shall be the head, and thou shalt be the tail.**

The so called Negros take their money to the stranger (Gentiles), which makes jobs available for their people, while the so called Negros remain unemployed we have the highest unemployment rate in the country despite a "good economy". Only in the Black community do you find every other ethnic group running the businesses, example: The Jewish people own everything the CURRENCY EXCHANGES, BANKS AND LENDING INSTITUTIONS. The Arabs own the GROCERY STORES, & FAST FOOD RESTAURANTS. The Asians own the CLOTHING STORES, NAIL SALONS AND BEAUTY SALONS. The East Indians own the CONVENIENT STORES AND GAS STATIONS. The White Caucasian owns the rest, and Hebrews Israelites own little if any businesses in our community.

> **Deuteronomy 28:45 Moreover all these curses shall come upon thee, and shall pursue thee, and overtake thee, till thou be destroyed; because thou hearkenedst not unto the voice of the LORD thy God, to keep his commandments and his statutes which he commanded thee:**

Deuteronomy 28:46 And they shall be upon thee for a sign and for a wonder, and upon thy seed for ever.

No matter where the children of Israel go or what they do these curses are going to be upon them. They are not keeping the Most High laws which he commandment them to do. Israel in the United States has long forgotten the laws of the Most High and this is the sole reason why they have been in this terrible condition since our arrival here. No matter how hard they try, they never get it right. The Most High said the curses are on Israel for a sign. A sign is an Indication; the Most High uses the curses to indicate who his true people are.

Deuteronomy 28:47 Because thou servedst not the LORD thy God with joyfulness, and with gladness of heart, for the abundance of all things;

Deuteronomy 28:48 Therefore shalt thou serve thine enemies which the LORD shall send against thee, in hunger, and in thirst, and in nakedness, and in want of all things: and he shall put a yoke of iron upon thy neck, until he have destroyed thee

The so called Negros of American oppressors literally put yokes of iron around their necks when they brought us here as captives. A yoke means a shaped piece in a garment, fitted about or below the neck and shoulders or about the hips, from which the rest of the garment hangs. They still have an iron yoke around their necks today. The word yoke also means agency of oppression, subjection, servitude and slavery. Iron is synonymous with power, and strength. Our oppressors have subjected and kept us in a powerful oppression and servitude.

Deuteronomy 28:49 The LORD shall bring a nation against thee from far, from the end of the earth, as swift as the eagle flieth; a nation whose tongue thou shalt not understand;

The far Nation spoken of in prophecy is the western hemisphere, particularly the United States. If you look on any map of the world and look at the so called mid-east, then look at the U.S. not only is the United States far from the mid-east, but it is actually at the end of the earth. Scripture mention this nation is swift as an eagle fly. It's not a coincidence that the national symbol for the U.S. is the eagle. When the slave traders and catchers came upon the shores of West Africa, the Hebrews didn't understand their languages. The so called Negroes had no knowledge of English or the various other languages the slave traders spoke. In the slave narrative by the slave Olaudah Equiano He tells of his first encounter with European slave traders. This is what he said:

"Their Complexions Too, different so much from ours, their long hair, and the Language they spoke, which was very different from any I had ever heard".

Deuteronomy 28:58 If thou wilt not observe to do all the words of this law that are written in this book, that thou mayest fear this glorious and fearful name, THE LORD THY GOD;

Deuteronomy 28:59 Then the LORD will make thy plagues wonderful, and the plagues of thy seed, even great plagues, and of long continuance, and sore sicknesses, and of long continuance.

These verses are clearly stating that Israel is always going to be a sick and disease stricken people. The so called Negros is only 12% of the U.S. general population, but they have the highest rate of cancer in the U.S. They lead in 8 out of the top 10 cancers. Hebrew Israelites men have the highest rate of prostate cancer in the world, for every 100,000 Hebrew men 185 will get prostate cancer. They are 4x's as likely to get disease as whites and 2x's as likely as Hispanics. They also have the highest rates of HEART DISEASE, DIABETES, HIGH BLOOD PRESSURE, SICKLE CELL ANIMA, STROKES, THYROID TUMORS, ASTHMA, LUPUS, & STD'S (sexually Transmitted Diseases).

> *Deuteronomy 28:62 And ye shall be left few in number, whereas ye were as the stars of heaven for multitude; because thou wouldest not obey the voice of the LORD thy God.*
>
> *Deuteronomy 28:63 And it shall come to pass, that as the LORD rejoiced over you to do you good, and to multiply you; so the LORD will rejoice over you to destroy you, and to bring you to nought; and ye shall be plucked from off the land whither thou goest to possess it.*
>
> *Deuteronomy 28:64 And the LORD shall scatter thee among all people, from the one end of the earth even unto the other; and there thou shalt serve other gods, which neither thou nor thy fathers have known, even wood and stone.*

In verses 64 the true Hebrew Israelites have been scattered from East to West North to South. There probably isn't a country on earth where Hebrew Israelites don't represent some percent of the population. The Hebrews can't be back in the land of Israel as a sovereign nation right now, and at the same time breaking the laws of AHAYAH. This is why the Hebrews Israelites (12 tribes) of the Western Hemisphere are here today in America. In the Countries where Israel is going to be scattered, they are going to serve all kinds of strange gods.

> ***Deuteronomy 28:65 And among these nations shalt thou find no ease, neither shall the sole of thy foot have rest: but the LORD shall give thee there a trmbling heart, and failing of eyes, and sorrow of mind:***

In verse 65 it states that among those nations where the children of Israel have been scattered we would find no ease or rest for our feet. Here in the Western Hemisphere the Hebrew Israelites have found no ease or peace, but rather horror and terror. Ralph Ginsberg documents some of the terror Hebrew Israelites have suffered in the United States in his book, 100 Years of Lynching.

> ***Deuteronomy 28:66 And thy life shall hang in doubt before thee; and thou shalt fear day and night, and shalt have none assurance of thy life:***

What it means is that the so called Negreos has feared for their lives since the time of slavery, it is a historical fact that their life has never had any value in this country. This is the reason for centuries, the so called Negros has been murdered and terrorized and no one can seem to stop it. Their lives hang in the balance before them. All the statistics show that they die from violence in the prime of our lives, more than any other ethnic group. In 1990 Hebrew Israelites represented 50% of the 23,760 murder victims known to police. The homicide rate among Hebrew men is generally 6 to 7 times higher than the rate among gentile men. The U.S. Department of Health and Human Services reported that in 1990.

> *Deuteronomy 28:67 In the morning thou shalt say, Would God it were even! and at even thou shalt say, Would God it were morning! for the fear of thine heart wherewith thou shalt fear, and for the sight of thine eyes which thou shalt see.*
>
> *Deuteronomy 28:68 And the LORD shall bring thee into Egypt again with ships, by the way whereof I spake unto thee, Thou shalt see it no more again: and there ye shall be sold unto your enemies for bondmen and bondwomen, and no man shall buy you.*

The so called Negros and the 12 Tribes were brought over here in America (Babylon) on Ships. In Deuteronomy 28:68 it is clear. Once we were over here we were sold and no man would save us. When it says "*And the LORD shall bring thee into Egypt again with ships*" notices the key word again, the word Egypt means bondage. In Exodus 13:3 proves that Egypt means Bondage. American today is spiritual Egypt, in Revelation 11:8 prove that American is spiritual Egypt. When it says "*and there ye shall be sold unto your enemies for bondmen and bondwomen, and no man shall buy you.*" The word bondmen means male slave, the word bondwomen means female slave. Also it says "*no man shall buy you*" what that means is that no man will redeem or save the children of Israel out of their condition that they are in. In a narrative by Friday Jones he explains his account of being sold as a Slave on page 9. In his narrative called Days of Bondage, Being a Brief Narrative of His Trials and Tribulations in Slavery. This is what he said:

> **"In 1856 my, wife and three children were for sale. I was for sale also. My two oldest children were sold—we were all the property of Dr. Ben Rogers then. Seven other of his servants were for sale, but he refused to sell any of them to a trader, either letting them select homes for themselves or he selecting one for them. He was pressed for $10,000—his youngest son got into a difficulty and he had to give a $10,000 bond. He forged $1,000 on the Wilmington N.C., Bank. Jno. O'Neil, of Raleigh, saw my wife and I in Raliegh, and told me to see my master and get him to sell them to him (O'Neil) and it would be a home for them for their life-time. See what a lie a man will tell. A short time after that he sold my wife and youngest child for as much as he gave for the four."**

Since the days that the Most High has brought the children of Israel forefathers out of the land of Egypt even unto this day they have been disobedient to the Father. They have stopped their ears from hearing his voice, and that's why all these evil has come and cleaved unto them as people. They are poor can't get ahead and are in a terrible state as a Nation. They are in America (aka Babylon) and other countries serving other gods and following their own imagination of their wicked hearts. This can be show in the following scriptures below:

Baruch 1:19-22: **Since the day that the Lord brought our forefathers out of the land of Egypt, unto this present day, we have been disobedient unto the Lord our God, and we have been negligent in not hearing his voice.**

20 Wherefore the evils cleaved unto us, and the curse, which the Lord appointed by Moses his servant at the time that he brought our fathers out of the land of Egypt, to give us a land that floweth with milk and honey, like as it is to see this day.

21 Nevertheless we have not hearkened unto the voice of the Lord our God, according unto all the words of the prophets, whom he sent unto us:

22 But every man followed the imagination of his own wicked heart, to serve strange gods, and to do evil in the sight of the Lord our God.—1611 KJV Bible (Apocrypha)

Just look at their conditions today. But the Most High said although we have forgotten about him and their special covenant with him. He has not forgotten about us, these curses will be lifted soon and a remnant of Israel shall be saved, I will explain this in the next section.

Enslavement

The children of Israel has been enslaved and sold by the Egyptians, the Muslims and the white Europeans and all the other nations. First let's start with Jacob (Israel) son Joseph. Joseph was already in Egypt and his brothers sold him to the Ishmaelite, because they were jealous of the love that their Father (Jacob) had for him (Genesis 37:3-36). Joseph was also highly favored by the Pharaoh of Egypt. A new Pharaoh arose up and didn't know Joseph nor did he show patronage to the children of Israel. The children of Israel begin to multiply rapidly and then a new King over Egypt enslaved the children of Israel and made them serve them with rigor as pointed out in these scriptures below:

> *Exodus 1:8-14 Now there arose up a new king over Egypt, which knew not Joseph.*
>
> *9 And he said unto his people, Behold, the people of the children of Israel are more and mightier than we:*
>
> *10 come on, let us deal wisely with them; lest they multiply, and it come to pass, that, when there falleth out any war, they join also unto our enemies, and fight against us, and so get them up out of the land.*
>
> *11 Therefore they did set over them taskmasters to afflict them with their burdens. And they built for Pharaoh treasure cities, Pithom and Raamses.*
>
> *12 But the more they afflicted them, the more they multiplied and grew. And they were grieved because of the children of Israel.*
>
> *13 And the Egyptians made the children of Israel to serve with rigour:*

14 And they made their lives bitter with hard bondage, in morter, and in brick, and in all manner of service in the field: all their service, wherein they made them serve, was with rigour.

Moses, who was a Hebrew, led the Hebrew Israelites out of Egypt in the wilderness (read Exodus chapter 3 to the end of Exodus chapter 14). At this point once the children of Israel were in the wilderness they started to sin against the Most High. The children of Israel were enslaved by the Muslims and the white Europeans also. The European involvement in the slave trade to America lasted over 3 centuries. The Muslim (Arabs) slave trade lasted 14 centuries and still exists in some parts of the world. Two out of three Hebrew Israelites slaves brought to American was men used for agricultural work. Two out of three were women were enslaved and by the white Europeans and the Muslims for sexual exploitation, concubine, harems, and for military services. Slaves that were transported across the Atlantic about 95% went to Central and South America, Portuguese, French, and Spanish possession. The other 5% went to the United States and that 5% consented of the tribe of Judah who are the so called Negros and the tribe of Gad who are the North American Indians.

During the Trans-Atlantic slave trade Europeans didn't have to venture into the jungles of Africa to capture the Hebrew Israelites because they were already sold into slavery by the African chief or by the Muslim slave traders at the coast. The Trans-Atlantic slave trade had three guilt partners; the African Chief's, the Muslim Arabs and the white Europeans.

A Remnant of Israel shall be saved

As I previously pointed out, the children of Israel were scattered because of their disobedient to the Most High. They were scacatered from Jerusalem and fled into the mountains of Africa during the destruction of Jerusalem in 70 A.D. by the Romans. The Most High never totally destroyed the children of Israel despite their disobedient and being rebellious towards him. That's why the Father promised to save a remnant. Here are some scriptures that prophecies speak about the Most High plan to save a remnant of Israel:

> **Romans 9:27 Esaias also crieth concerning Israel, Though the number of the children of Israel be as the sand of the sea, a remnant shall be saved:**

Only a remnant of the children of Israel shall be saved and that remnant is those in the latter (end of days) times who will turn to the Father again and serve him in truth and righteousness and those that that the Father put his spirit upon to wake them (children of Israel) up to understand who they really are and who serve him In truth and righteousness will also be a part of that remnant.

> **Isaiah 6:13 But yet in it shall be a tenth, and it shall return, and shall be eaten: as a teil tree, and as an oak, whose substance is in them, when they cast their leaves: so the holy seed shall be the substance thereof.**

Only a tenth shall return out of Israel/12 Tribes. A small remnant reserved, that number being put indefinitely. This also links back to Zechariah 13:8 where it says that a *"third shall be left therein."* that is the remnant that will be left out of Israel.

Isaiah 10:20-22 And it shall come to pass in that day, that the remnant of Israel, and such as are escaped of the house of Jacob, shall no more again stay upon him that smote them; but shall stay upon the Most High, the Holy One of Israel, in truth.

21 The remnant shall return, even the remnant of Jacob, unto the mighty God.

22 For though thy people Israel be as the sand of the sea, yet a remnant of them shall return: the consumption decreed shall overflow with righteousness.

In Isaiah 11:11 we read that all of the People of Israel (12 Tribes) will be gathered from the above places mentioned in scripture. This is a future prophecy. The prophet Ezekiel also identifies this remnant of Israel:

Ezekiel 37:11-12 Then he said unto me, Son of man, these bones are the whole house of Israel: behold, they say, Our bones are dried, and our hope is lost: we are cut off for our parts.

12 Therefore prophesy and say unto them, Thus saith the Lord GOD; Behold, O my people, I will open your graves, and cause you to come up out of your graves, and bring you into the land of Israel.

Ezekiel 37:21-24 And say unto them, Thus saith the Lord GOD; Behold, I will take the children of Israel from among the heathen, whither they be gone, and will gather them on every side, and bring them into their own land:

22 And I will make them one nation in the land upon the mountains of Israel; and one king shall be king to them all: and they shall be no more two nations, neither shall they be divided into two kingdoms any more at all:

23 Neither shall they defile themselves any more with their idols, nor with their detestable things, nor with any of their transgressions: but I will save them out of all their dwellingplaces, wherein they have sinned, and will cleanse them: so shall they be my people, and I will be their God.

24 And David my servant shall be king over them; and they all shall have one shepherd: they shall also walk in my judgments, and observe my statutes, and do them.

The 37 chapter of Ezekiel is speaking about the children of Israel who were driven away from their homelands. Yet the Most High did not completely destroy them.

4

Religion

MUCH CONFUSION EXISTS regarding different religious beliefs. My research and through biblical facts has lend me to come to these conclusion about these religions. In this chapter I will be covering Christianity, Jehovah Witness and Muslims. Many of the children of Israel are stuck in these religion and they are serving other gods as prophecy has already foretold us. My intent and wishes are not to offend anyone, but to shed light about these religions to name a few on how they keep the Most High people from truly serving him. All the prophets in the Bible taught that there was one God, and that is the God of Israel (AHAYAH AHSER AHAYAH—I AM THAT I AM). So if the Most High prophets taught that it is one true God, and then we must ask this question, why is it so many different religions? That's why the first Commandment is very important, and it is read like this:

> *Exodus 20:3 Thou shalt have no other Gods before me.*

The Most High God tells us to not have any other gods before him. What we must understand is that there is only one true God as I have already stated (Psalm 96:4-5). When we are in these religions it is important to know that each religion have their own gods (idols). Majority of Christians will tell you that Christianity is a religion that is derived from Jesus (Yashaya); one must ask the question is that true? The answer to that is No. The Bible identifies the Messiah as a Jew (Tribe of Judah) (John 4:9-10). Jesus (Yashaya) kept the laws of the Most High like: the Passover, the Sabbath, the Dietary Law and other Holy days. In Christianity they teach and tell the people that they don't have to keep the laws of the Most High and that the laws are done away with. We must keep the laws of the Most High, as it is written in:

> **Matthew 5:17-18 Think not that I am come to destroy the law, or the prophets: I am not come to destroy, but to fulfil.**
>
> **18 For verily I say unto you, Till heaven and earth pass, one jot or one tittle shall in no wise pass from the law, till all be fulfilled.**
>
> **Baruch 4:1 This is the book of the commandments of the Most High, and the law that endureth for ever: all they that keep it shall come to life; but such as leave it shall die.**

Why do they say that Christianity comes from Jesus (Yashaya) and majority of Christians don't even keep the laws of the Most High? Especially the children of Israel (12 Tribes). I would also like to point out that the word Christ was never apart of Jesus name. Christ means 'anointed one' it is pronounced in the Greek as 'Christos' since the New Testament was written in Greek as I pointed out previously in the book. So now we can see why the Roman Catholic Church would add that to the name to further deceive you to believe this is his name when it's not.

I would like to start off by saying Christianity is not the truth. It's full of Lies and Deception. This is the world largest religion and it has deceived our people far too long. We need to understand that everything you see and hear is not always true. I just pray and hope that you really get the message that I am trying to convey to you. I repeat Christianity is full of lies and deception. They teach that the creator or the God of Israel doesn't have a name and his name is God. The Father gave us his name. This can be pointed out in Exodus chapter 3 when Moses asks the Most High what he shall tell the children of Israel his name was:

> ***Exodus 3:13-15 And Moses said unto God, Behold, when I come unto the children of Israel, and shall say unto them, The God of your fathers hath sent me unto you; and they shall say to me, What is his name? what shall I say unto them?***
>
> ***14 And God said unto Moses, I AM THAT I AM: and he said, Thus shalt thou say unto the children of Israel, I AM hath sent me unto you.***
>
> ***15 And God said moreover unto Moses, Thus shalt thou say unto the children of Israel, The LORD God of your fathers, the God of Abraham, the God of Isaac, and the God of Jacob, hath sent me unto you:***

this is my name for ever, and this is my memorial unto all generations.

Moses asks the Most High, what shall he say to the children of Israel when he goes to the children of Israel and say "*The God of your fathers hath sent me unto you*" and the Most High said "*I AM THAT I AM*: and he said, "*Thus shalt thou say unto the children of Israel,* **I AM** *hath sent me unto you.*" The Father true name in Hebrew is **AHAYAH ASHAR AHAYAH** *(AHAYAH—I AM)*. Notice in verse 15 he said "*this is my name forever*," So if this is the Father true name one must ask the question to why don't Christianity call upon the Creator or the Most High true name. We see that God is not his name; in fact the word God is pagan and can also mean an idol. The Old Testament was written in Hebrew and the New Testament in Greek. Also you can find the father true name in the JPS Hebrew-English Tanakh. Remember Hebrew is read from right to left and in the Ancient Hebrew there are no e soundings.

I would also like to point out that in Christianity they call upon the Son (the Messiah) Name as "Jesus". That is a roman Greek god named Iēsous. The Messiah real name in Hebrew is Yashaya which mean in the Hebrew salvation, saving. What we must understand is that we know from the previous chapter that the Messiah was a Hebrew Israelites. The letter J is the newest letter in the English alphabet. Also there is no J sound in the Ancient Hebrew language let along the letter J. So if the letter J is the newest letter in the alphabet and the Messiah was a Jew from the tribe of Judah (Hebrews 7:14) then his name can't be Jesus (Iesous) that is a Greek name and they (Roman Catholic Church) put it into English form, it's not a Hebrew name. I would like to prove my case with this scripture:

> **Acts 26:14 And when we were all fallen to the earth, I heard a voice speaking unto me, and saying in the Hebrew tongue, Saul, Saul, why persecutest thou me? it is hard for thee to kick against the pricks.**

In Acts 26:14 we read that Paul heard Jesus (Yashaya) speak to him in the Hebrew tongue. The messiah was a Black Jew from the tribe of Judah as stated in Hebrews 7:14 as I pointed out previously. This means that if the Messiah spoke Hebrew and was from the Tribe of Judah then his name must be Hebrew as well. The Messiah true name is YASHAYA in the Ancient Hebrew tongue as I pointed out. Yashaya means salvation, saving, safety, liberty, and deliverance.

Many so called Christians and as well as others think that Jesus (Yashaya) died on an actual cross. Long before the Christian era, crosses were used by the ancient Babylonians as symbols in their worship of the fertility god Tammuz. The indisputable sign of Tammuz, the mystic Tau of the Babylonians and Egyptians, was brought into the Church chiefly because of Constantine. We know through the divine scriptures that the messiah was hanged on a Tree because he was a Hebrew Israelites from the tribe of Judah, because the children of Israel were told to hang a man on a tree if he has committed a sin worthy of death. This is shown in this scripture below:

> **Deuteronomy 21:22-23 And if a man committed a sin worthy of death, and he be to be put to death, and thou hang him on a tree:**
>
> **23 His body shall not remain all night upon the tree, but thou shalt in any wise bury him that day; (for he that is hanged is accursed of God) that thy land be**

not defiled, which the Lord thy God giveth thee for an inheritance.

In verse 22 it is clear to us that if a man committed a sin worthy of death, then he is to be hanged on a tree. Here are more scripture to prove that he was hanged on a tree:

Acts 5:30 The God our fathers raised up Jesus, whom ye slew and hangd on a tree.

1 Peter 2:24 Who his own self bare our sins in his own body on the tree, that we, being dead to sins, should live unto righteousness: by whose stripes ye were healed

Acts 13:29 And when they had fulfilled all that was written on him, they took him down from the tree, and laid him in a sepulchre.

It clearly points out that the Messiah was hanged on a tree. Peter clearly says that Jesus (Yashaya) bare our sins in his own body on a <u>Tree</u>. It is also clear that once Jesus (Yashaya) had passed over (died) they took his body from the tree a placed it in a tomb. Also another thing that I would like to point out is that most of the so called Negros and other 12 Tribes are unaware why they go to church (Congregation/Assembly) on Sunday which is the first day of the week; I will further go into more detail within this chapter. I must also point out that the Roman Catholic Church inserted the word Church into the KJV Bible. In place of the word church it was supposed to say, congregation or Assembly. They also inserted the word virgin, in place of the word virgin it supposed to be young maiden or maiden. What we must understand is that the so called Negroes never had a Religion and Christianity was forced upon the slaves when they got off slave ships and onto the plantation. The slaves were forced to go to church and thus becoming brainwashed and ripped from their heritage.

There has been a strong delusion within the church (Congregation) about the Rapture Doctrine. Many so called Christians believe in this false doctrine and don't fully understand who is behind it. My research as lead me to uncover those who had a part in spreading this false doctrine to deceive the masses. I will go into a little history as to who is behind the Rapture doctrine. The "Rapture" teaching was not taught by the early Church, it was not taught by Church of the first centuries, it was not taught by the Reformers, it was not taught by anyone (except a couple of Roman Catholic theologians) until about the year 1830. At the time of the Reformation, the early Protestants widely held and were convinced the Pope was the supreme individual embodiment and personification of the spirit of antichrist, and the Roman Church, the Harlot System of Revelation seventeen. This understanding was responsible for bringing millions of believers out of the Roman Catholic religious system. John Nelson Darby is responsible for the spreading and teaching of the Rapture doctrine, along with his other Plymouth Brethren. Edward Irving (1792-1834), a Scottish Presbyterian and forerunner of the Pentecostal and Charismatic movements, translated Lacunza's work from Spanish into English in a book titled *The Coming of Messiah in Glory and Majesty with a Preliminary Discourse,* published in London in 1827 by L.B. Seeley & Sons. His church in London seated one thousand people and was packed week after week with a congregation drawn from the most brilliant and influential circles of society.

Irving discovered Lacunza's book and was deeply shaken by it. At this time Irving heard what he believed to be a voice from heaven commanding him to preach the *Secret Rapture of the Saints.* Irving then began to hold Bible conferences throughout Scotland, Emphasizing the coming of the Messiah to rapture His Church. About this same time there began the emergence of a new movement which came to be known as the *Plymouth Brethren.* A man by the name of John Nelson Darby was the leading spirit among the Plymouth Brethren from 1830 onward. Darby was from a prosperous Irish family, was educated as a lawyer, took high honors at Dublin University, and then turned aside, to his father's chagrin, to become a minister. John Nelson Darby (1800-1882), Irving and Darby were contemporaries, though associated with different spiritual movements. Another series of meetings were in progress at this time. A Church of Ireland clergyman, later with the Plymouth Brethren, also promoted Futurism and a secret rapture. Darby's biographers refer to him as *"the father of dispensationalism."* And the crown jewel in the kingdom of dispensationalism is, of course, the so-called SECRET RAPTURE! Darby, called the 'father of dispensationalism', was responsible for the widespread dissemination of the new and novel pretribulation doctrine beginning around 1830 through his ministry in the Plymouth Brethren movement. The doctrine soon spread to America and was widely popularized by the Scofield Reference Bible. The rapture doctrine, it began as a Roman Catholic invention. The Jesuit priest *Ribera's* writings influenced the Jesuit priest *Lacunza,* Lacunza influenced *Irving,* Irving influenced *Darby,* Darby influenced *Scofield,* Scofield and Darby influenced *D. L. Moody,* and Moody influenced *the Pentecostal Movement.*

It is also important to point out that allot of the Most High chosen people (Hebrew Israelites/Jews) are part of a false religion called Jehovah witness. I must also point out that this religion is based on mind control just like that others are. In fact the Founder of this occult organization was a 33rd Degree Free Mason. The founder of this religion is Pastor Charles Taze Russell. He was also a 33rd Degree Mason. He also believed it was appropriate to lie to opposers. He didn't see anything wrong with being a Mason while at the same time a so call Christian. He also co-published The Herald of the Morning magazine, with its founder, N. H. Barbour. This magazine was to so call foretells the coming of Christ in 1874. Russell is part of the Russell bloodline of the Illuminate, which also founded the infamous Skull and Bones Society. My desires are not to talk about the founder or slander his name, but to shed light to the readers about this false mean spirited religion. Charles T. Russell, the founder of the Jehovah's Witnesses, would indicate that he had ties with the Masons. He used Masonic symbols. The Watchtower drawing that graced early publications right up to a couple of Decades ago was pure Masonic. Other Masonic symbols were used frequently on his publications.

Russell also believed in the Masonic belief of a "New World Order". Russell believed in Masonry until his death, as evidence by the Masonic gravestone that he lies beneath. He also told his followers to read the book, Angels and Women". This was a book dictated about a "fallen Angels" (demon) to a women spirit medium. Those who are a part of this false and evil religion I would advise you to do more research before you just start to follow a man made up religion. In a speech that Pastor Russell gave at a Special 1913 Convention Report of the International Bible Students. Under the subject of "The Temple of God" is a discourse by Pastor Russell reported verbatim on pages 120 these words:

> **"I am very glad to have this particular opportunity of saying a word about some of the things in which**

we agree with our Masonic friends, because we are speaking in a building dedicated to Masonry and we also are Mason. <u>I am a free a accepted Mason</u>, If I may carry the matter to its full length, because that is what our <u>Masonic brethren</u> like to tell us, that they are free and accepted Mason. That is there style of putting it. Now I am a free an accepted Mason. I trust we all are, but not after the style of our Masonic Brethren. We have no qaurall with them. I am not going to say a word against Masons, and I can appreciate that there are certain very precious truths that are held in part by our Masonic friends. I have talked to them at times, and they have said, How do you know about all of these things? We thought nobody knew about all of these things expect those who had access to our very highest logic"

The Founder(s) of this false religion even built a mansion for the Prophets in the Bible. They thought all the prophets in the bible were coming back soon in 1878. The mansion was called the, Beth Sarim that they built. The ungodly has mixed the Gospel of truth and Masonry. The most deceptive teachings are those that have mixed truth with error. I can only pray that this information will find its way too many modern day Jehovah's Witnesses who revere this false prophet and his twisted teachings. I pray many eyes will be opened and modern so called Jehovah's Witnesses will begin an investigation into their roots. The Most High chosen people especially needs to come out of this false religion.

There are many of the children of Israel who is a part of a false Religion known today as being a Muslim. As I pointed out in the book previously under the section called "Enslavement" that the Muslims bought and sold the children of Israel. How is it that the so called Negros (Tribe of Judah /Jews) and the rest of the 12 Tribes follow a religion that was never meant for them and founded by Arabs? They follow these so called man made up religions is due to them being lost and not knowing who they are (Jeremiah 17:4), but really religion confuses the people even more. Although Islam is today a monotheist religion, its roots are in paganism. Islam is a religious system that begun in the 7th century by Muhammad. Muslims follow the teachings of the Qur'an and strive to keep the Five Pillars. Muhammad had many male and female slaves. He used to buy and sell them, but he purchased more. "Al-ilah" was later shortened to Allah before Muhammad began promoting his new religion in 610 AD.

Allah is the Arabic word for "God" used by Muslims. I would like to address that Islam worship the Moon. Moon worship has been practiced in Arabia since 2000 BC. The crescent moon is the most common symbol of this pagan moon worship as far back as 2000 BC. In Mecca, there was a god named **Hubal** who was Lord of the Kabah. There is evidence that Hubal was referred to as "Allah". If you look on many of the temples you will see a moon crescent symbol and the Nation of Islam religious symbol is a crescent moon. The children of Israel have defiled themselves with this religious and many others. This is prophecies that they would go and worship the other gods and the hosts of heaven:

> **Deuteronomy 17:3 And hath gone and served other gods, and worshipped them, either the sun, or moon, or any of the host of heaven, which I have not commanded;**

> **Jeremiah 8:2 And they shall spread them before the sun, and the moon, and all the host of heaven, whom they have loved, and whom they have served, and after whom they have walked, and whom they have sought, and whom they have worshipped: they shall not be gathered, nor be buried; they shall be for dung upon the face of the earth.**

These two scriptures above lets us know that the children of Israel would go and serve other gods. In Islam they worship a black Stone, called the black Stone of Mecca or the Kaaba stone, it's a Muslim relic. It is the eastern cornerstone of the Kaaba, the ancient sacred stone building towards which Muslims pray, in the center of the Grand Mosque in Mecca, Saudi Arabia. The pilgrims circle the Kaaba as part of the Tawaf ritual of the Hajj, many of them try, and if possible, to stop and kiss the Black Stone, emulating the kiss that it received from the Islamic prophet Muhammad. The Black Stone of Kaaba or Mecca in Arabic is called *Al-hajar Al-aswad.* The word Kaaba—Ka'ba—Ka'bah means Cube. This is also mentioned in the Holy Scripture that the children of Isarel would go and serve other gods, and a stone is one of them:

> **Deuteronomy 29:17 And ye have seen their abominations, and their idols, wood and stone, silver and gold, which were among them :)**

It is clear that the Nation of Islam (Muslims) worship a Stone, The Kaaba is nothing more but a stone, the children of Israel was warned, but they worshiped it anyway. They (Muslims) believe that this stone fell from the sky during the time of Adam and Eve, and that it has the power to cleanse worshippers of their sins by absorbing them into itself. They say that the Black Stone was once a pure and dazzling white and it has turned black because of the sins it has absorbed over the years. I would also like to point out that it is remarkable, however, that even though the temple contained 360 idols worshipped before Muhammad's Prophet Hood, the black stone was never kissed or made an idol of worship. In fact, the Ka'ba was never worshipped by the idolaters prior to Muhammad's Prophet Hood. The building contained idols of worship but the building itself was never an object of worship.

The Understanding Of John 3:16

It is very important to point out that Majority of Christianity like to quote John 3:16 and don't understand what's really being said. Religious intuitions teach that the Most high, the God of Israel loves everybody, this is true to those who serve him in truth and righteousness and reverence his people who are the children of Israel (12 Tribes). Salvation is to the Jews, what that means is that all nations must come to the true Jews to receive salvation (Acts 13:47), because the Most High only gave Israel his words (Romans 3:1-4). I will further discuss the duty of the Most High people later in the book. I will provide a full breakdown of what John 3:16 really means:

> ***John 3:16 For God so loved the world, that he gave his only begotten Son, that whosoever believeth in him should not perish, but have everlasting life.***

For the Most High so love the world, this seems like it is talking about the whole world and all the Nations. The word world means 'A <u>particular class of people</u>, with common interests, aims, etc.'

> **John 17:9 I pray for them: I pray not for the world, but for them which thou hast given me; for they are thine.**

The Messiah says that he "*pray for them and not the world*". The Messiah said he pray not for the world. The <u>them</u> are the Hebrew Israelites/Jews in which he was sent to redeem them for their sins.

> **John 6:37-39 All that the Father giveth me shall come to me; and him that cometh to me I will in no wise cast out.**
>
> **38 For I came down from heaven, not to do mine own will, but the will of him that sent me.**
>
> **39 And this is the Father's will which hath sent me, that of all which he hath given me I should lose nothing, but should raise it up again at the last day**.

In John 6:39 it says "<u>that of all which he hath given me</u>" meaning there is a different between everybody in the Earth and a group of people that the Most High gave to the Messiah and that group of people is the Children of Israel. Then it goes on and gives us a clue to who those people are, when it says "<u>but should raise it up again</u>". That word <u>again </u>is very important, because of that people who the Father gave the Messiah his Son he will raise them (Hebrew Israelites) up again in the last days. In order to be raised up again you had to be up at one point before then taken down. You can't be raised up again if you were never up in the first place. Let's continue to read for more understanding.

Deuteronomy 7:6 For thou art an holy people unto the Lord thy God: the Lord thy God hath chosen thee to be a special people unto himself, above all people that are upon the face of the earth.

This is Moses speaking to the Children of Israel. It says "above all people that are upon the face of the earth". The word above mean, up. So we see that the children of Israel were set up above all the people upon the face of the earth by the Most High, because the Most High chose them to give his laws to. The Nation of Israel received these blessing, but later on fell as a nation due their disobedient.

Acts 1:6 When they therefore were come together, they asked of him, saying, Lord, wilt thou at this time restore again the kingdom to Israel?

The disciple as the Messiah this question "Lord, wilt thou at this time <u>restore again the kingdom to Israel</u>?" Israel was the Nation that was up but fell and that needed to be restored again, that's why the Messiah said in John 17:9 "<u>*I pray for them: I pray not for the world,*</u>" And in John 6:39 he said "<u>*but should raise it up again at the last day*</u>", meaning raise the Nation of Israel back up again. We know that John 3:16 isn't talking about everybody in the World, it's talking about a group of people. Look at the Definition for the word world. The word world means 'A <u>particular class of people</u>, with common interests, aims, etc.' Since we know that the word world also means a Particular class of people, with common interests, and aims know we can understand why the Messiah said in John 17:9 "I pray for <u>them</u>: I pray not for the world, the <u>them</u> is the Nation of Israel". Also the words restore means 'To bring back into existence, use, or the like; reestablish'.

> **Acts 5:30-31 The God of our fathers raised up Jesus, whom ye slew and hanged on a tree.**
>
> **31 Him hath the God exalted with his right hand to be a Prince and a Saviour, for to give repentance to Israel, and forgiveness of sins.**

According to verse 31 the Messiah came to take away the sins of Israel. Please read the Precepts to Matthew 1:21, Ephesians 1:17, and Colossians 1:14, to see that he came to take away the sins of Israel. The whole conclusion of John 3:16 when it says *"For the Most High so loved the world"* this cant mean everybody its talking about a specific group of people. That's why the Messiah said this:

> **Matthew 5:24 But he answered and said, I am not sent but unto the lost sheep of the house of Israel.**

That specific group of people is the Children of Israel.

The Change Of The Sabbath

It's very important to know the true day of the Sabbath. In Christianity they teach that the Sunday is the Sabbath when in fact it's Saturday. The Romans themselves admired the religion and culture of Greece. They adopted Greek gods and blended them into their own religions. The result was a mixture of ancestor worship, emperor worship, and sun worship, a religion that included not one god, but many. The Jews, on the other hand, worshipped only one God, the God of Israel (AHAYAH). Though surrounded by the images of Greek and Roman deities, they served other gods and it lead to them rebelling against the God of Israel as I mentioned earlier in the book.

In the Old Testament, the Most High established the Sabbath as the celebration of His creative work and as a day of freedom from labor and it was a sign between the children of Israel. On the Sabbath there is no work to be done, sex, buying, it's a Holy day a day of rest. See scripture below:

Genesis 2:2-3 And on the seventh day the God ened his work which he had made; and he rested on the seventh day from all his work which he had made.

3 And God blessed the seventh day, and sanctified it: because that in it h had rested from all his work which God created and made.

Christianity was not the only religion that was gaining popularity within the Roman Empire. Various forms of sun worship were also attracting adherents, among who were the emperors themselves. There had been other forms of sun worship that were also in vogue. When Nero commissioned a gigantic statue in his own honor, it featured a likeness of the emperor's head in sun-god fashion. Known as the Colossus of Nero, it stood 37 meters high. Future emperors would alter the features dedicate it to the "unconquerable sun." Aurelian, emperor from 270-275 AD, established a state religion that included worship of the emperor and the sun. Constantine was, like Aurelian, a worshiper of the sun. He was also the first Emperor to profess belief in Christianity, and shall I say the founder also of this false religion. Constantine's personal religion was a mixture of Mithraic sun worship and Christianity. According to his Christian biographer, Eusebius, he taught all his armies to zealously honor the Lord's Day—Sunday—referring to it as "the day of light and of the sun." This was distinctly pagan terminology.

The Roman Catholic Church changed the Original Sabbath of the Bible to Sunday in 321 (A.D.). Emperor Constantine on March 7, 325 (A. D.) issued the first civil legistration proclaiming Sunday, the venerable day of the Sun, a day of rest. What we must understand is that this is prophecy that the Roman Catholic Church would change the Sabbath day (Day7) to Sunday (Day 1), due to them worshipping the Sun. Here is the scripture to prove this:

> *Daniel 7:25 And he shall speak great words against the most High, and shall wear out the saints of the most High, and think to change times and laws: and they shall be given into his hand until a time and times and the dividing of time.*

The is part of the Ten Commandments, the Sabbath is to be remembered and kept as a Holy day:

> *Exodus 20:8 Remember the sabbath day, to keep it holy.*
>
> *Exodus 31:12-17 And Lord spake unto Moses, saying,*
>
> *13 Speak thou also unto the children of Israel, saying, Verily my sabbaths ye shall keep: for it is a sign between me and you throughout your generations; that ye may know that I am the Lord that doth sanctify you.*
>
> *14 Ye shall keep the sabbath therefore; for it is holy unto you: every one that defileth it shall surely be put*

to death: for whosoever doeth any work therein, that soul shall be cut off from among his people.

15 Six days may work be done; but in the seventh is the sabbath of rest, holy to the Lord: whosoever doeth any work in the sabbath day, he shall surely be put to death.

16 Wherefore the children of Israel shall keep the sabbath, to observe the sabbath throughout their generations, for a perpetual covenant.

17 It is a sign between me and the children of Israel for ever: for in six days Ahayah made heaven and earth, and on the seventh day he rested, and was refreshed.

This is a sign between the children of Israel (Jews/12 Tribes of Israel).

5

The Most High Chosen People

As I POINTED out before the Hebrew Israelites are the Most High chosen people. They were chosen to teach the word of the Most High. They are sent to be a light to the Gentiles; I will speak more about this in the next chapter. The Most High chosen people are a Holy people, so holy that they were set apart from the other Nations. They were given Laws, Statutes, and commandments. I will give a breakdown down through scripture to show how holy the children of Israel are:

> **Deuteronomy 4:7-8 For what nation is there so great, who hath God so nigh unto them, as the Lord our God is in all things that we call upon him for?**
>
> **8 And what nation is there so great, that hath statutes and judgments so righteous as all this law, which I set before you this day?**

Moses asked the children of Israel 2 question he said "For what nation is there so great and what nation is there so great, that hath statutes and judgments as righteous as all this law". They are as holy as a people that as a Nation we are the only people that have Statutes laws and judgments.

> **Deuteronomy 7:6-8 For thou art an holy people unto the Lord H thy God: the Lord thy God hath chosen thee to be a special people unto himself, above all people that are upon the face of the earth.**
>
> **7 The Lord did not set his love upon you, nor choose you, because ye were more in number than any people; for ye were the fewest of all people:**
>
> **8 But because the Lord loved you, and because he would keep the oath which he had sworn unto your fathers, hath the Lord brought you out with a mighty hand, and redeemed you out of the house of bondmen, from the hand of Pharaoh king of Egypt.**

The children of Israel are a special people and above all the people (Gentiles) upon the face of the earth. In verse 8 it said that the Most High loved them, the 12 Tribes of Israel and delivered our forefathers out of the hand of the Egyptians.

> **Matthew 5:13-14 Ye are the salt of the earth: but if the salt have lost his savour, wherewith shall it be salted? it is thenceforth good for nothing, but to be cast out, and to be trodden under foot of men.**

14 Ye are the light of the world. A city that is set on an hill cannot be hid.

The children of Israel (Hebrew Israelites) are the salt of the world, the so called Negros and the rest of the 12 Tribes. They are the ones that give the world flavor. The children of Israel are great at anything they do, like playing sports, and entertainment. The Hebrew Israelites (children of Israel) are the best at what they do, that's why it says they are the salt of the world.

Leviticus 20:24-26 But I have said unto you, Ye shall inherit their land, and I will give it unto you to possess it, a land that floweth with milk and honey: I am the Most High your power, which have separated you from other people.

25 Ye shall therefore put difference between clean beasts and unclean, and between unclean fowls and clean: and ye shall not make your souls abominable by beast, or by fowl, or by any manner of living thing that creepeth on the ground, which I have separated from you as unclean.

26 And ye shall be holy unto me: for I the Most High am holy, and have severed you from other people, that ye should be mine.

In Leviticus 20:24-26 that the children of Israel are so holy that they are separated from the other people (Gentiles) in the world. Also they are told to put a different between clean and unclean animals;

this lets us know that they have a Holy dietary law to follow (Leviticus 11:1-47). The 12 Tribes are to be Holy for the Most High is Holy and he has severed them from other people that they should be his own.

Conclusion

The children of Israel are meant to be a light to the Gentiles so that they may also obtain salvation and the keeping of the law. The Hebrew Israelites are the Most High servant as a Nation and they are to do his will and walk righteously as he is righteous.

> *2 Esdras 7:10-11 And I said, It is so, Lord. Then said he unto me, Even so also is Israel's portion.*
>
> *11 Because for their sakes I made the world: and when Adam transgressed my statutes, then was decreed that now is done.*
>
> *2 Esdras 6:55-56 All this have I spoken before thee, O Lord, because thou madest the world for our sakes*
>
> *56 As for the other people, which also come of Adam, thou hast said that they are nothing, but be like unto spittle: and hast likened the abundance of them unto a drop that falleth from a vessel.*

They are so holy and precious that the world was made for the children of Israel sake. It's important that the Most High people walk, talk, and keep the Most High's ways, so they can store up good works in Heaven and show their Faith with works.

6

The Jewish People

THE SO CALLED Jewish people over in Israel today who proclaim they are the real Jews are not, they are Khazars (white Europeans/Caucasians). I would like to also point out that they are High priest, sorcery, and wizards on a High level, they wear all Black from head to toe. They don't even believe in Jesus (yashaya) that can be pointed out in the Talmud (Jewish bible). They are from Esau descendants the brother of Jacob. Esau is the father of the white Edomites as I point in the previously chapter. Khazars are Japhetic in origin and converted to Judaism over the centuries. At that time Cordoba was the splendor of Moorish Spain (a mixture of black skinned Muslims and Israelites), and was the main center of European Culture. In his letter to Hasdai, King Joseph stated that he was from the line of Japheth, from the seed of Togarmah, and Japheth's grandson. He further stated that Togarmah, who was the brother of Ashkenaz, had ten sons and the Khazars represented the seventh son. With his own lips, this King had given the root of his being and the lineage of his offspring which was from the sons of Japheth. Here are the sons of Japheth:

Genesis 10:2-5** **2** **The sons of Japheth; Gomer, and Magog, and Madai, and Javan, and Tubal, and Meshech, and Tiras.

3 And the sons of Gomer; Ashkenaz, and Riphath, and Togarmah.

4 And the sons of Javan; Elishah, and Tarshish, Kittim, and Dodanim.

5 By these were the isles of the Gentiles divided in their lands; every one after his tongue, after their families, in their nations.

According to the King of the Khazars, his people descended from the family of Magog. Like all European nations at the time. However, ca. 740 C.E. King Bulan initiated the conversion of his kingdom to a new and different philosophy. Before the conversion, the Kagan invited representatives of Christianity, Islam and the Israelites to discuss the three doctrines. It was unanimously agreed, in response to the Kagan's question, that the doctrine of the Israelites was closest to the truth. And also in order for the Khzars to remain independent they chose the faith that neither the Christian or Muslims was part of but both respected. After the conversion the Khazar King changed his name to become King Obadiah. They displayed much hope but very little understanding, especially of spiritual matters. They had to invent their own brand of the law which later they named Judaism. The word "Judaism" cannot be found in the writings of the Prophets of old, neither is it found anywhere in the Holy Scriptures. Judaism is a misunderstanding or perversion of the customs of the ancient Israelites, as practiced by the Khazars. The edomites participated in the Roman War of 66-70 A.D. Arthur Koestler in his book "*THE THIRTEENTH TRIBE*" gives further detailed information about the Khazars and their conversion and how the majority of today's European Jews are direct descendants of them. The information contained in his book is backed up by scripture that shows the Jewish people over in Israel today are Gentiles, not natural born Hebrew Israelites. This is what he said:

> **According to Microsoft Encarta, "Today, about 85% of all Jews are Ashkenazim". The Ashkenazi are not descendants of Israel, Ashkenaz was the grandson of Japheth and brother of Togarmah. Arthur Koestler further explains why today's Jews call themselves Ashkenazi even though they are the Physical seed of Togarmah.**

Aruthur Koestler shows that the Khazars took on the name of Ashkenaz because it was prophesied in the Holy Scriptures (Jeremiah 51:27). The Ashkenaz and their allies would conquer Babylon. This is what the Messiah had to say about them:

> **Revelation 2:9 I know thy works, and tribulation, and poverty, (but thou art rich) and I know the blasphemy of them which say they are Jews, and are not, but are the synagogue of Satan.**

> **Revelation 3:9 Behold, I will make them of the synagogue of Satan, which say they are Jews, and are not, but do lie; behold, I will make them to come**

and worship before thy feet, and to know that I have loved thee.

The messiah said they are the synagogue of Satan. This lets us know that the real Jews are in poverty and in tribulation, and we can examine this by their condition today. Then it goes on to say, but they are rich, the real Jews are rich, they are rich spiritually and physically, but once they disobeyed the God of Israel they were stripped of their physically possessions. I agree with Arthur Koestler research. This is from page 17 of his book the "*The Thirteenth Tribe*":

> **The large majority of surviving Jews in the world are of Eastern European descent — and thus perhaps mainly of Khazar origin. If so, this would mean that their ancestors came not from the Jordan but from the volga, not from Canaan but from the Caucasus, once believed to be the cradle of the Aryan race; and that genetically they are more closely related to the Hun, uigur, and Magyar tribes than to the seed of Abraham, Isaac, and Jacob**.

The Israelites came from Canaan through the lineage of Abraham, Isaac and Yaaqob; while the Khazars came from the Caucasus through Gomer, Togarmah and Khazar, and the Edomites from Mount Seir through Abraham, Isaac and Esau or Edom.

Conclusion

The Hebrew Israelites descended from Jacob (Israel); while the Khazars descended from Japheth and the Edomites from Esau. The Israelites originated from northeastern Africa; while the Khazars originated from southeastern Europe and the Edomites from the southern Palestine/Jordan area. The Majority of Hebrew Israelites have black skin, according to the Holy Scripture, with woolly hair. The Israelis who are over in the land today have white skin, mostly blue eyes, long straight hair. The Hebrew Israelites (Jews) spoke Egyptian, Hebrew, Aramaic and later Greek, Roman, Spanish, various West African languages and today the various languages of the Americas. The Khazars (Israelis) spoke a language called Yiddish which many of them still speak still till this day. They are now in possession of the land known as Palestine. They (Khazars) have become known as the true biblical tribe over the centuries. The Jewish people over in the land today and around the world are being lied to. Allot of them are not even Jewish, they were put on films and other documents going into Israel to fulfill the prophecies. Allot of the Jewish people don't even believe in Judaism.

The Star Of David Deception

So what is the symbol known as the Star of David? It is the triangle that is the primary focus in all Illuminati realms, whether in the ritual ceremonies of the Rosicrucians and Masons or the witchcraft, astrological and black magic practices of other Illuminist followers. In almost every instance of occultism, the triangle is used among Satanists and witches, the double triangle, and the quote on quote Seal of Solomon, also called the hexagram, is reverence highly. This seal is actually composed of two triangles, superimposed on each other. The hexagram is one of the most powerful symbols of the occult, is used by witches to cast spells. Known more for being the Israeli symbol the Star of David—it is important to note that the Zionist organization adopted it as a symbol for the flag of Israel in 1897 which pre-dates its use in Freemasonry. Six triangles is the Egyptian hieroglyphic for the

Land of the Spirits, in which this (6-pointed star) was the first sign or hieroglyphic of Amsu. In the Astro-Mythology of the Egyptians. The Zionism (Jewish Khazars) knew that in these end times that the chosen people (children of Israel/Jews) of the Most High that would wake up and come into the knowledge that they are the Chosen people of the living God. So upon our people waking up, they would run right back into worship of the idolatry they served while in bondage in Egypt, the Most High never gave the children of Israel a star to worship, neither to wear it around their necks as some due today. This can be pointed out in the Holy Bible:

> **Amos 5:26 But ye have borne the tabernacle of your Moloch and Chiun your images, the star of your god, which ye made to yourselves.**

The Most High never gave the children of Israel a star, he gave them laws and statutes and commandments, and they themselves followed the heathens and made unto themselves a star unto a false god. They fell victim to the magical powers of this Star which was worshipped in Egypt, while they were wandering in the wilderness.

> **Acts 7:43 Yea, ye took up the tabernacle of Moloch, and the star of your god Remphan, figures which ye made to worship them: and I will carry you away beyond Babylon.**

The children of Israel (Hebrew Israelites/Jews) worshiped this Star that was not given unto to hem by the Most High. They took it upon themselves in disobedience to follow the gods of the heathens, therefore making them a Star unto their God to be worshipped. The

Jewish (Khazars) people whom the Messiah identified as the synagogue of Satan, use this star and worship this false god they don't believe in the Most High, the God of Israel, they worship Satan. So the symbols they put forth is the representation of Satan, and by the chosen people upholding this pagan idolatry, they fail to come into the full understanding that the Most High.

7

Duty Of The Chosen People

THE NATION OF Israel is known as the chosen people, but scholars and others never say what they are chosen to do. The bible is very clear about the job of Israel and the reason they were chosen. The Israelites are not the only ones to gain salvation (Romans 11:11), but it was and is their job to teach the world the truth about the heavenly father and his laws. This is why in Acts 10: the angel told Cornelius the Italian to go to Peter the Hebrew Israelite, so he might tell him what he ought to do. Peter taught Cornelius the full law of the God of Israel (Acts 10:33). The job of Israel is to teach the world the ways of the Most High. The children of Israel were given the oracle (word) of the Most High:

> **Romans 3:1-4 What advantage then hath the Jew? or what profit is there in circumcision?**
>
> **2 Much every way: chiefly, because that unto them were committed the oracles of God.**

3 For what if some did not believe? shall their unbelief make the faith of Ahaya without effect?

4 God forbid: yea, let God be true, but every man a liar; as it is written, that thou mightest be justified in thy saying and mightest overcome when thou art judged.

The children of Israel are the servants of the Most High and must do all of his services here on earth. One of those services is to go out into the world as priest and teach the other nations (Gentiles) about the Most High (AHAYAH). Some scholars are teachers would argue that the Most High cast away his people. I would like to say that isn't true. Israel is his servant and he has not casted away his people and they are to be a light to the Gentiles:

Isaiah 41:8-9 But thou, Israel, art my servant, Jacob whom I have chosen, the seed of Abraham my friend.

9 Thou whom I have taken from the ends of the earth, and called thee from the chief men thereof, and said unto thee, Thou art my servant; I have chosen thee, and not cast thee away.

Acts 13:47 For so hath the Lord commanded us, saying, I have set thee to be a light of the Gentiles, that thou shouldest be for salvation unto the ends of the earth.

Romans 11:1-2 *I say then, Hath God cast away his people? God forbid. For I also am an Israelite, of the seed of Abraham, of the tribe of Benjamin.*

2 *God hath not cast away his people which he foreknew. Wot ye not what the scripture saith of Elias? how he maketh intercession to God against Israel, saying,*

Throughout biblical times and even now, Israel (12 Tribes) has become a spiritually dead people as I pointed in the previous chapters that they would discontinue from their heritage (Jeremiah 17:4). In the past and today, they have become accustomed to mixing the pure worship of the God of Israel (AHAYAH) with that of pagan idol gods (religion). In the process of doing this they continue to bring more curses down on them, and at the same time have lost the knowledge that Most High has given them. Even at the second coming of the messiah, which is the times we are in, the end times, Israel will be used to bring the world into the truth. As it is written in:

Zechariah 8:23 *Thus saith the LORD of hosts; In those days it shall come to pass, that ten men shall take hold out of all languages of the nations, even shall take hold of the skirt of him that is a Jew, saying, We will go with you: for we have heard that God is with you.*

All nations are going to come to the children of Israel because at this time the world will have knowledge of who they are and what their purpose. The children of Israel hold the keys of salvation.

Conclusion

The children of Israel are the only people who have been called the sons (children), servants, priest, chosen and the inheritance of the Most High. He never called any other group of people these things, but this doesn't mean that the other nations (Gentiles) are not welcome to have salvation; also the Gentiles are referred to as heathens, as written in these scriptures:

> *2 Esdras 2:34-37 And therefore I say unto you, O ye heathen, that hear and understand, look for your Shepherd, he shall give you everlasting rest; for he is nigh at hand, that shall come in the end of the world.*
>
> *35 Be ready to the reward of the kingdom, for the everlasting light shall shine upon you for evermore.*
>
> *36 Flee the shadow of this world, receive the joyfulness of your glory: I testify my Saviour openly.*
>
> *37 O receive the gift that is given you, and be glad, giving thanks unto him that hath led you to the heavenly kingdom.*—Apocrypha Books (1611 KJV)
>
> *Romans 1:16 For I am not ashamed of the gospel of Christ: for it is the power of God unto salvation to everyone that believeth; to the Jew first, and also to the Greek.*

All people, of all languages and races are welcome to be partakers of the truth, and obtain the reward of everlasting life, But ALL that want truth and salvation must come to Israel to get that truth and salvation. For this is the whole duty of the children of Israel, is to be a light to the Gentiles as I stated.

Bibliography

Equiano, Olaudah, and Robert J. Allison. *The interesting narrative of the life of Olaudah Equiano*. Boston: Bedford Books Of St. Martin's Press, 1995.

Koestler, Arthur. The *thirteenth tribe: the Khazar empire and its heritage*. New York: Random House, 1976.

Soukhanov, Anne H.. *Encarta world English dictionary*. New York: St. Martin's Press, 1999.

Days of bondage autobiography of Friday Jones being a brief narrative of his trials and tribulations in slavery. Electronic ed. Chapel Hill, N.C.: Academic Affairs Library, University of North Carolina at Chapel Hill, 1999. Print.

The Holy Bible. 1611 King James Bible

The Temple of God, a discourse by Pastor Russell given at the 1913 covention of international Bible student. See (Pg. 120-125)

JEREMY G. SHORTER was born in Atlanta, Georgia, and lived in the inner city. He graduated from high school in 2008 and later started seeking work in the film industry. While out of school he started during research on his true heritage. In the course of his research, he has uncovered startling evidence indicating that his true heritage stems back to the ancient Biblical Hebrew Israelites. He later went on to create a website called, Israelites Unite, while researching, he found out about himself and his people. Later on he compiled all the research that he had from his site and decided to publish a book about his findings. He quoted from his book, *"My motive for writing this book is to enlighten the truth about the history and heritage of the so called Negroes of America and the 12 Tribes who are scattered throughout the world. Our true and rich heritage that has been hidden from us throughout generation to generation, which has been suppressed by the school system, religious intuitions, scholars, and many more to keep our people from knowing their true Nationality."*

Mr. Shorter loves to teach his people who they really are so they can became and shine like that bright light that they are. For more information about his research and work, visit his website at: www.IsraelitesUnite.com.

NOTES

NOTES

NOTES

NOTES

NOTES

NOTES

NOTES

NOTES

NOTES

NOTES

NOTES